A POET TO HIS BELOVED

I bring you with reverent hands
The books of my numberless dreams,
White woman that passion has worn
As the tide wears the dove-grey sands,
And with heart more old than the horn
That is brimmed from the pale fire of time:
White woman with numberless dreams,
I bring you my passionate rhyme.

William Butler Yeats

MODERN
LOVE
POEMS

ILLUSTRATED BY HANS ERNI

EDITED BY D. J. KLEMER

Doubleday & Company, Inc.
Garden City, New York

The editor and publisher are grateful to the following publishers and individuals for permission to include in this volume the selections listed below:

CHARLES G. BELL for "The Fire," copyright © 1960 by The Curtis Publishing Company. Reprinted by permission of the author.
THE BOBBS-MERRILL COMPANY, INC. for "When in the Crowd I Suddenly Behold," from A Cedar Box, by Robert Nathan. Copyright © 1929, 1956, used by special permission of the publishers.
JOHN CIARDI for "Most Like an Arch This Marriage," copyright © 1958 by John Ciardi; "Men Marry What They Need. I Marry You," copyright © 1958 by John Ciardi; "To Judith Asleep," copyright © 1949, 1950, 1955, 1958 by John Ciardi. Reprinted by permission of the author.
THE JOHN DAY COMPANY, INC. for "For Eros (II)" from Bright Ambush, by Audrey Wurdemann. Copyright 1934 by Audrey Wurdemann. Reprinted by permission by the publisher.
DODD, MEAD & COMPANY for "Love," "The Wayfarers," "The Hill," "One Day," from The Collected Works of Rupert Brooke. Copyright 1915 by Dodd, Mead & Company, Inc. Copyright 1943 by Edward Marsh. Reprinted by permission of Dodd, Mead & Company, McClelland and Stewart Limited and Sidgwick & Jackson Limited.
DOUBLEDAY & COMPANY, INC. for "How Strange Love Is in Every State of Consciousness," copyright © 1958 by Delmore Schwartz, first published in Mutiny. From the book Summer Knowledge, by Delmore Schwartz. "Part of Plenty" from the book Aegean Island & Other Poems, by Bernard Spencer. Copyright 1946 by Bernard Spencer. "Spoils," originally appeared in The New Yorker, from the book The Collected Poems of Robert Graves, published by Doubleday & Company, Inc. and Messrs. Cassell & Company, Limited. Copyright © 1955 by Co-Productions Roturman S. A. Reprinted by permission of Roturman S. A.
NORMA MILLAY ELLIS for "Never May the Fruit Be Plucked," "Modern Declaration," and Sonnet XXX, from Fatal Interview. From The Collected Poems of Edna St. Vincent Millay.
FABER AND FABER LTD. for "Of the Unscathing Fire" and "News of the World," from The Nine Bright Shiners, by Anne Ridler.
HARCOURT, BRACE AND WORLD, INC. for "Sonnets—Unrealities I." Copyright 1923, 1951, by E. E. Cummings. Reprinted from Poems 1923–1954 by E. E. Cummings. "The Sleepers," from These Times, by Louis Untermeyer. Copyright 1917 by Henry Holt and Company; copyright 1945 by Louis Untermeyer. "Counting," "Explanations of Love," from Good Morning, America, by Carl Sandburg. Copyright 1928, 1956, by Carl Sandburg. "Home Thoughts," from Smoke and Steel, by Carl Sandburg. Copyright 1920 by Harcourt, Brace and World, Inc.; renewed, 1948, by Carl Sandburg. "Another Song," from Once in a Blue Moon, by Marion Strobel. Copyright 1925 by Harcourt, Brace and World, Inc.; renewed, 1953 by Marion Strobel. "The Dark Chamber," "Burning Bush," from Burning Bush, by Louis Untermeyer. Copyright 1928 by Harcourt, Brace and World, Inc.; renewed, 1948, by Louis Untermeyer. "Hands," from The New Adam, by Louis Untermeyer. Copyright 1920 by Harcourt, Brace and World, Inc.; renewed, 1948 by Louis Untermeyer. "A Simile for Her Smile," from Ceremony and Other Poems, by Richard Wilbur. Copyright 1948, 1949, 1950, by Richard Wilbur.

PREFACE

What is love? Certainly it is different things to different people, and it has been variously defined by the poets represented in this collection. To some it is passion; to others it is a fairly awesome thing. "How strange love is . . ."; "it is a fever and a stir, a leaping siren in the blood, a torturing delight." Audrey Wurdemann sees love as "a candle to burn a little while against the dark," and Marion Strobel reflects that it is "a beauty made to wonder at and not to grasp." Others have found it easier to define what love is not. Edna St. Vincent Millay muses, "It is not all; it is not meat or drink." And Rolfe Humphries obviously agrees, for he writes that "love, out of season, is a poor food." Unhappily, the aftermath of love can also be synonymous with bitterness: "the winter of love is a cellar of empty bins, in an orchard soft with rot." Although the poets disagree as to whether love is a thing to be praised, savored, or lamented they would certainly all be in accord with Robert Frost, who says:

> *Earth's the right place for love:*
> *I don't know where it's likely to go better.*

This, then, is a book about love—a volume dedicated to love in all its seasons.

Unlike so much of the current trend in the arts—be it painting, music, literature, or drama—the poems in this collection are neither obtuse, harsh, discordant, jangling, nor full of abstract imagery. Each poem has been included here because it is intelligible, and because it represents love in beautiful words. These are poems that sing! This is a book for lovers in all moods and, I hope, for lovers of all ages.

D. J. Klemer

MODERN LOVE POEMS

THE FIRE

The fire was slow kindling—it was damp wood,
Old, and moistened by the earth and rain.
Two times I rose to mend it from your side,
Stirred the wet sticks and blew the smoldering ends.
Then in the clear cold night and clearing of the wood,
We two, under the stars, hearts not young,
And wet with time's worse rain, forgot the fire—

Until suddenly it was there, each kindled point
Enforcing another, to take us by surprise,
A brightness huge and fierce, a living flame,
That sent up sparks to coil among the stars—
Earth's poor matter assaulting the night skies,
A trembling moment of eternity . . .
That was the constellation of our love.

We lay afterward a long time
On the plain ground—earth where we are bred.
And watched the lattice of transfigured wood
Slough films of gray ash and renew its glowing;
And in the cleared space of the dew-cold forest,
Saw now and then how a few last sparks would rise
To their brief ecstasy among the stars.

Charles G. Bell

I did not see the iris move,
I did not feel the unfurling of my love.

This was the sequence of the flower:
First the leaf from which the bud would swell,
No prison, but a cell,
A rolled rainbow;
Then the sheath that enclosed the blow
Pale and close
Giving no hint of the blaze within,
A tender skin with violet vein.
Then the first unfurling petal
As if a hand that held a jewel
Curled back a finger, let the light wink
Narrowly through the chink,
Or like the rays before the sunrise
Promising glory.

And while my back is turned, the flower has blown.
Impossible to tell
How this opulent blossom from that spick bud has grown.
The chrysalis curled tight,
The flower poised for flight—
Corolla with lolling porphyry wings
And yellow tiger markings
A chasing-place for shade and light:
Between these two, the explosion
Soundless, with no duration.
        (I did not see the iris move,
        I did not feel my love unfurl.)
The most tremendous change takes place in silence,
Unseen, however you mark the sequence,
Unheard, whatever the din of exploding stars.

Anne Ridler

I SHALL BE LOVED AS QUIET THINGS

I shall be loved as quiet things
Are loved—white pigeons in the sun,
Curled yellow leaves that whisper down
One after one;

The silver reticence of smoke
That tells no secret of its birth
Among the fiery agonies
That turn the earth;

Cloud-islands; reaching arms of trees;
The frayed and eager little moon
That strays unheeded through a high
Blue afternoon.

The thunder of my heart must go
Under the muffling of the dust—
As my grey dress has guarded it
The grasses must;

For it has hammered loud enough,
Clamored enough, when all is said:
Only its quiet part shall live
When I am dead.

Karle Wilson Baker

THE SLEEPERS

Moonlight and music and the sound of waves
Reached out and held us there;
Each close to each,
Upon the night-blurred and deserted beach.
She sang an old, imperishable air
Softly . . . and from forgotten graves
A mist of memories arose
As if in answer to an unspoken call.
A soft and intimate breeze
Crooned over us and over all
The blue and faintly-singing spaces;
Over the quiet and the salty balm,
Over the velvet skies and seas,
Over our half-concealed and cloudy faces.
That strange and rosy wind
Mellowed the distance; smoothing down the thinned,
Sharp edges of the sickle-moon;
Bringing the night so close
That when our fingers clasped
We grasped and held its greatness and calm
Warmly within each palm.

And, as her head drooped back,
And the breath of the world came slower,
A drowsy voice grew out of the black
Night as her voice sank lower.
Something caught her unspoken word,
It answered and mingled with her;
Their breathing blended and I heard
The voice of Sleep and her sleepy voice
Sing together . . .

The wind crept up on the sands and stopped;
The voices dropped.
Our fingers loosened; the night imposed
The weight of all sleepers upon us and closed
Our heavy eyes.

Then, as we lay,
I stretched my arm into the skies
And plunged it through that shining spray,
Pushing my shoulders through the cloudy bars,
And grasped the moon like a scythe.
I flung my swaying body in a lithe
And rhythmic play,
Cutting down great, wide swathes of stars;
Reaping the heavens with a blithe
Song till the blue fields were bare.
Then, when the last gold bud was shaken free
And all the silver flowers of the night
Had rained and heaped about her there,
I threw the bright blade into the sea . . .

There was a hissing and an end of light.
And we slept—dreamlessly.

Louis Untermeyer

OUT

Let's go play in the sun
you and I, hand in hand on the beaches
. . . at night, over our whispers, hear the sea.
Let's look into the light,
smiling, squinting our eyes;
      you can shake out your hair
O, into the salt and gleaming wind
and we shall not go back, not look inside,
      Close up the starless closet, throw the key.
Let's drop all thoughts, all deaths, all duties;
Let's, clean as a shell, like the sand blown free
be tossed spendthrift, become pure and bare,
      become so shining that we cease to be.

Nathaniel Burt

NIGHTSONG

Beside you,
lying down at dark,
my waking fits your sleep.

Your turning
flares the slow-banked fire
between our mingled feet,

and there,
curved close and warm
against the nape of love,

held there,
who holds your dreaming
shape, I match my breathing

to your breath;
and sightless, keep my hand
on your heart's breast, keep

nightwatch
on your sleep to prove
there is no dark, nor death.

Philip Booth

DREAM

I had returned from dreaming—
When there came the look of you
And I could not tell after that,
And the sound of you
And I could not tell,
And at last the touch of you
And I could tell then less than ever,
Though I silvered and fell
As at the very mountain-brim
Of dream.

For how could the motion of a shadow in a field
Be a person?
Or the flash of an oriole-wing
Be a smile?
Or the turn of a leaf on a stream
Be a hand?
Or a bright breath of sun
Be lips?

I can reach out and out—and nothing will be there . . .
None of these things are true.
All of them are dreams—
There are neither streams
Nor leaves nor orioles nor you.

Witter Bynner

AUGUST NIGHT

Shadow like a liquid lies
   in your body's hollows
In your eyes garnet stars
   shift their facets with your breath
The August night in Nubian
   something green mixed with the dark
a powder for your skin that tints
   the implications of your bones
with copper light
   an aura round your knees your navel
a little pool with pulsing tide

Is there beauty deeper than your cool
   form drawn by the occult stylus
of this night
   slanting to autumn
the long dawn soon bringing wrappings
   for your breast?
Has any other watchman stiller stayed
   to the smiting of this gong
half in glory half afraid to look
   at what obscure in light
is now explained by shade?

May Swenson

BURNING BUSH

And suddenly the flowing night stands still
    And the loose air grows tense and small;
Runners of flame from nowhere rise and fill
    The narrowest veins, till all

The martyrdom of fire is not enough
    For bodies eager to be doomed;
Burning in one long agony of love,
    Burning but not consumed.

And the last white blaze leaps from our being's core
    And flesh, too shaken to rejoice,
Cries out till quiet, vaster than before,
    Speaks in the still, small voice.

Louis Untermeyer

LOTUSES

Deliver me, O beloved, from this evil
Of possessing you too near my hungry side
Or my hands or my lips, undo my passionate purpose
Of knowing you, become again as wide
As the night is, be wonderful with unknown stars
Far from the rim of touch, and hold so deep
A quietness that down the dim lake of heaven
We float away on lotuses of sleep.

Witter Bynner

THE HOUNDED LOVERS

Where shall we go?
Where shall we go
    who are in love?

Juliet went
to Friar Laurence's cell
    but we have no rest—

Rain water lies on
the hard ground reflecting
    the morning sky

But where shall we go?
We cannot resolve ourselves
    into a dew

nor sink into the earth.
Shall we postpone it
    to Eternity?

The dry heads of the
golden rod
    turned to stiff ghosts

jerk at their stalks
signaling grave warning.
    Where shall we go?

The movement of benediction
does not turn back
    the cold wind.

William Carlos Williams

LEAVES BEFORE THE WIND

We have walked, looking at the actual trees:
The chestnut leaves wide-open like a hand,
The beech leaves bronzing under every breeze,
We have felt flowing through our knees
  As if we were the wind.

We have sat silent when two horses came,
Jangling their harness, to mow the long grass.
We have sat long and never found a name
For this suspension in the heart of flame
  That does not pass.

We have said nothing; we have parted often,
Not looking back, as if departure took
An absolute of will—once not again
(But this is each day's feat, as when
  The heart first shook).

Where fervor opens every instant so,
There is no instant that is not a curve,
And we are always coming as we go;
We lean toward the meeting that will show
  Love's very nerve.

And so exposed (O leaves before the wind!)
We bear this flowing fire, forever free,
And learn through devious paths to find
The whole, the center, and perhaps unbind
  The mystery

Where there are no roots, only fervent leaves,
Nourished on meditations and the air,
Where all that comes is also all that leaves,
And every hope compassionately lives
  Close to despair.

May Sarton

WHAT MUST (iii)

Lovers who must say farewell
When the road has reached the trees,
Lovers who have all to tell
Before the road runs out of sight
In the green beyond the leaves—
The green cove below the light,
Lovers who must say farewell
When the road has reached the trees,
Touching hand to hand to speak
All their love has ever known,
Find no words to speak and say
Love. . . . Oh love. . . .

        and, each alone,
Walk together toward the trees
Where the road runs out of sight
In the green beyond the leaves—
The green cove below the light.

Archibald MacLeish

THE WAYFARERS

Is it the hour? We leave this resting-place
    Made fair by one another for a while.
Now, for a god-speed, one last mad embrace;
    The long road then, unlit by your faint smile.
Ah! the long road! and you so far away!
Oh, I'll remember! but . . . each crawling day
Will pale a little your scarlet lips, each mile
    Dull the dear pain of your remembered face.

. . . Do you think there's a far border town, somewhere,
    The desert's edge, last of the lands we know,
      Some gaunt eventual limit of our light,
    In which I'll find you waiting; and we'll go
Together, hand in hand again, out there,
    Into the waste we know not, into the night?

Rupert Brooke

HOME THOUGHTS

The sea rocks have a green moss.
The pine rocks have red berries.
I have memories of you.

. . . .

Speak to me of how you miss me.
Tell me the hours go long and slow.

Speak to me of the drag on your heart,
The iron drag of the long days.

I know hours empty as a beggar's tin cup on a rainy day,
    empty as a soldier's sleeve with an arm lost.

Speak to me . . .

Carl Sandburg

RENDEZVOUS

If the deep night is haunted, it is I
Who am the ghost; not the tall trees
Nor the white moonlight slanting down like rain,
Filling the hollows with bright pools of silver.

A long train whistle serpentines around the hill
Now shrill, now far away.
Tell me, from what dark smoky terminal
What train sets out for yesterday?

Or, since our spirits take off and resume
Their flesh as travellers their cloaks, O tell me where,
In what age and what country you will come,
That I may meet you there.

Robert Hillyer

ONE DAY

Today I have been happy. All the day
   I held the memory of you, and wove
Its laughter with the dancing light o' the spray,
   And sowed the sky with tiny clouds of love,
And sent you following the white waves of sea,
   And crowned your head with fancies, nothing worth,
Stray buds from that old dust of misery,
   Being glad with a new foolish quiet mirth.

So lightly I played with those dark memories,
Just as a child, beneath the summer skies,
   Plays hour by hour with a strange shining stone,
For which (he knows not) towns were fire of old,
   And love has been betrayed, and murder done,
And great kings turned to a little bitter mould.

Rupert Brooke

LIGHTNING

There is a solitude in seeing you,
Followed by your presence when you are gone.
You are like heaven's veins of lightning.
I cannot see till afterward
How beautiful you are.
There is a blindness in seeing you,
Followed by the sight of you when you are gone.

Witter Bynner

At dawn she lay with her profile at that angle
Which, sleeping, seems the stone face of an angel . . .

DAYBREAK

THESE IMAGES REMAIN

Now that the evening gathers up the day,
All birds and trees and the delicious sum
Of scent and sound, of all instinctual play,
And hive-enclosed the bees' hurried hum,
I am so lonely for the commonplace,
The usual things of love, evenings and sleeps,
Multiple nights bringing the sound of wings,
Multiple mornings, every one for keeps,
I could almost despair of love that brings
So piercing a delight, so close to grief,
So full of absence that it learns to flourish
On a few hours, bearing a single leaf,
A single spring so great a tree to nourish;
On such a meagre piece of earth, the root
Hugging what shallow bed to bear what fruit?

Even such fervor must seek out an end,
Magnificent and wasteful though it be,
Even such fervor granted to ascend
Long stairs of light in a pure majesty
Of longing and desire, impassioned progress
That has no end within reality,
And so climbs on in careless loneliness
To look down on the sleeping human city,
Even such fervor must become so tired
It prays only a little place to creep;
A small real stone is more to be desired
Than all the world of light, an hour of sleep,
And those tears too expensive now that start
From radiant eyes and empty the whole heart.

May Sarton

31

EXPLANATIONS OF LOVE

There is a place where love begins and a place
    where love ends.

There is a touch of two hands that foils all
    dictionaries.

There is a look of eyes fierce as a big Bethlehem open hearth
    furnace or a little green-fire acetylene torch.

There are single careless bywords portentous as a
    big bend in the Mississippi River.

Hands, eyes, bywords—out of these love makes
    battlegrounds and workshops.

There is a pair of shoes love wears and the coming
    is a mystery.

There is a warning love sends and the cost of it
    is never written till long afterward.

There are explanations of love in all languages
    and not one found wiser than this:

There is a place where love begins and a place
    where love ends—and love asks nothing.

Carl Sandburg

SONNET

Love is not all: it is not meat nor drink
Nor slumber nor a roof against the rain;
Nor yet a floating spar to men that sink
And rise and sink and rise and sink again;
Love can not fill the thickened lung with breath,
Nor clean the blood, nor set the fractured bone;
Yet many a man is making friends with death
Even as I speak, for lack of love alone.
It well may be that in a difficult hour,
Pinned down by pain and moaning for release,
Or nagged by want past resolution's power,
I might be driven to sell your love for peace,
Or trade the memory of this night for food.
It well may be. I do not think I would.

Edna St. Vincent Millay

HOW STRANGE LOVE IS,
IN EVERY STATE OF CONSCIOUSNESS

How strange love is in every kind of consciousness:
How strange it is that only such gentleness
Begets the fury of joy and all its tenderness,
That lips and hands for all their littleness
Can move throughout the body's wilderness
Beyond the gaze of consciousness, however it towers
Possessed and blessed by the power which flowers as a fountain
   flowers!

Delmore Schwartz

IN TIME LIKE AIR

Consider the mysterious salt:
In water it must disappear.
It has no self. It knows no fault.
Not even sight may apprehend it.
No one may gather it or spend it.
It is dissolved and everywhere.

But out of water into air
It must resolve into a presence,
Precise and tangible and here.
Faultlessly pure, faultlessly white,
It crystallizes in our sight
And has defined itself to essence.

What element dissolves the soul
So it may be both found and lost,
In what suspended as a whole?
What is the element so blest
That there identity can rest
As salt in the clear water cast?

Love in its early transformation,
And only love, may so design it
That the self flows in pure sensation,
Is all dissolved and found at last
Without a future or a past,
And a whole life suspended in it.

The faultless crystal of detachment
Comes after, cannot be created
Without the first intense attachment.
Even the saints achieve this slowly;
For us, more human and less holy,
In time like air is essence stated.

May Sarton

SONG FROM THE GULF

Love from a source admired
Gives a fine pleasure,
Music and measure
Sweetly combining,
Sweet to the sense:
Who, in her senses,
Who, in his mind,
Wants other token
Once having taken
Seizure of this?

Some, who lack choosing,
Drink a dark water,
Brackish and bitter,
Drawn from a shrinking pool,
Salt as the sea:
Love, out of season,
Is a poor food,
But, duly taken,
By the same token,
Sustenance is.

Rolfe Humphries

NEWS OF THE WORLD

Love is our argument of joy,
Its cadence is the tierce de picardy;
Early love is the rare, thin
May-day hymn
Sun-rising from the river tower.

And what are love's infallible signs?
A clutch of fear as someone enters;
Dumb darkness when he is gone;
But in between
The night-blowing Cereus breaks into flower

And all the constellations bless.
Such a calm and glow of glory
In his presence, that distress
Seems meaningless:
So gay, serene, supreme his power.

Anne Ridler

LOVE BELEAGURED

This the last refuge I can give you
Yet you will find no peace, not even here.
Nor in the solace of my arms that hold you,
You will find no safety anywhere.

Perhaps for moments, perhaps forgetting
The clamor of anger that rages across the sky
You will believe that here, in tenderness begetting
Comfort for your heartache is peace. That is a lie.

Love is not a drug for endless sleeping.
It is not quiet for one raidless night.
Love is a fever and a stir, a leaping
Siren in the blood, a torturing delight.

And if you come to me, come with this knowing,
O my dear, the unrest is mine. It is upon me; I wait
With all the whistles of destruction blowing,
To share this last joy, sweet and desperate.

Katherine Garrison Chapin

AT A WINDOW

Give me hunger,
O you gods that sit and give
The world its orders.
Give me hunger, pain and want,
Shut me out with shame and failure
From your doors of gold and fame,
Give me your shabbiest, weariest hunger!

But leave me a little love,
A voice to speak to me in the day end,
A hand to touch me in the dark room
Breaking the long loneliness.
In the dusk of day-shapes
Blurring the sunset,
One little wandering, western star
Thrust out from the changing shores of shadow.
Let me go to the window,
Watch there the day-shapes of dusk
And wait and know the coming
Of a little love.

Carl Sandburg

EPITAPH

Say he was sad, for there was none to love him,
And sing his song.
Now he is still, and the brown thrush above him
Sings all day long.

Say he was lost, for there was none to find him,
And hold him tight.
Now the brown hands of mother earth will mind him
All through the night.

Robert Nathan

LUCK

Sometimes a crumb falls
From the tables of joy,
Sometimes a bone
Is flung.

To some people
Love is given,
To others
Only heaven.

Langston Hughes

NEED

What do we need for love—a midnight fire
Flinging itself by fistfuls up the chimney
In soft bright snatches? Do we need the snow,
Gentle as silence, covering the scars
Of weeks of hunger, years of shabby having?
Summer or winter? A heaven of stars? A room?
The smiling mouth, the sadness of desire
Are everywhere the same. If lovers go
Along an unknown road, they find no less
What is familiar. Let them stay at home,
And all will still be strange. This they know
Who with each heartbeat fight the fear of change.

Babette Deutsch

SQUANDERINGS

Be aware
That goods are brittle,
That those who have little often break that little
While those who have much take care.

Love is not a wealth to scatter,
To forsake.
Loneliness is hard to break.
Squanderings matter.

Witter Bynner

NATURAL LAW

If you press a stone with your finger,
Sir Isaac Newton observed,
The finger is also
Pressed by the stone.
But can a woman, pressed by memory's finger,
In the deep night, alone,
Of her softness move
The airy thing
That presses upon her
With the whole weight of love? This
Sir Isaac said nothing of.

Babette Deutsch

"THOSE WHO LOVE"

Those who love the most,
Do not talk of their love.
Francesca, Guinevere,
Deirdre, Iseult, Heloise,
In the fragrant gardens of heaven
Are silent, or speak if at all
Of fragile, inconsequent things.

And a woman I used to know
Who loved one man from her youth,
Against the strength of the fates
Fighting in somber pride,
Never spoke of this thing,
But hearing his name by chance,
A light would pass over her face.

Sara Teasdale

LEGEND

Where are you hid from me, belovèd one
That I am seeking through the lonely world—
A wanderer, on my way home to you?
Dark is the night, and perilous the road;
At many a breast in longing have I leaned,
At many a wayside worshipped—and my heart
Is tired from long travelling. Perhaps
In centuries to come you wait for me,
And are, as yet, an iris by the stream,
Lifting her single blossom, or the soft
Tremulous haze upon the hills—and we
Have missed each other. Oh, if it be so,
Then may this song reach to the verge of doom,
Ages unborn—to find you where you are,
My lonely one—and like a murmuring string,
Faint with one music, endlessly repeat,
To you not even knowing I was yours,
Her plaintive burden from the dolorous past
Of dusty legend, her archaic woe—
Telling of one upon a hopeless quest,
How, in the dark of time, he lost his way.

John Hall Wheelock

DREAM GIRL

You will come one day in a waver of love,
Tender as dew, impetuous as rain,
The tan of the sun will be on your skin,
The purr of the breeze in your murmuring speech,
You will pose with a hill-flower grace.

You will come, with your slim, expressive arms,
A poise of the head no sculptor has caught
And nuances spoken with shoulder and neck,
Your face in a pass-and-repass of moods
As many as skies in delicate change
Of cloud and blue and flimmering sun.

         Yet,
You may not come, O girl of a dream,
We may but pass as the world goes by
And take from a look of eyes into eyes,
A film of hope and a memoried day.

                              Carl Sandburg

THE TREE IN PAMELA'S GARDEN

Pamela was too gentle to deceive
Her roses. "Let the men stay where they are,"
She said, "and if Apollo's avatar
Be one of them, I shall not have to grieve."
And so she made all Tilbury Town believe
She sighed a little more for the North Star
Than over men, and only in so far
As she was in a garden was like Eve.

Her neighbors—doing all that neighbors can
To make romance of reticence meanwhile—
Seeing that she had never loved a man,
Wished Pamela had a cat, or a small bird,
And only would have wondered at her smile
Could they have seen that she had overheard.

Edwin Arlington Robinson

THE REVELATION

I awoke happy, the house
Was strange, voices
Were across a gap
Through which a girl
Came and paused,
Reaching out to me—

Then I remembered
What I had dreamed—
A girl
One whom I knew well
Leaned on the door of my car
And stroked my hand—

I shall pass her on the street
We shall say trivial things
To each other
But I shall never cease
To search her eyes
For that quiet look—

William Carlos Williams

NEVER MAY THE FRUIT BE PLUCKED

Never, never may the fruit be plucked from the bough
And gathered into barrels.
He that would eat of love must eat it where it hangs.
Though the branches bend like reeds,
Though the ripe fruit splash in the grass or wrinkle on the tree,
He that would eat of love may bear away with him
Only what his belly can hold,
Nothing in the apron,
Nothing in the pockets.
Never, never may the fruit be gathered from the bough
And harvested in barrels.
The winter of love is a cellar of empty bins,
In an orchard soft with rot.

Edna St. Vincent Millay

THE WORLD NARROWED TO A POINT

Liquor and love
when the mind is dull
focus the wit
on a world of form

The eye awakes
perfumes are defined
inflections
ride the quick ear

Liquor and love
rescue the cloudy sense
banish its despair
give it a home.

William Carlos Williams

FOR EROS II

Who thinks love is a prize to put away
With spice and silk until the love be wasted,
Hoping the tender halcyon-hues will stay,
The silk not raveled and the spice untasted?
Such is the folly of the over-wise,
Who shield themselves against a golden spring,
And will not see the sun before their eyes,
And call the sweet blood-stirring no such thing.

Love should be spent while living; love's a candle
To burn a little while against the dark
Beyond our towering shadows; do not handle
And test and tease it long; be still, and mark
How even the tardiest one must pay his debt
When by the eager wick a spark is set.

Audrey Wurdemann

DIVINELY SUPERFLUOUS BEAUTY

The storm-dances of gulls, the barking game of seals,
Over and under the ocean . . .
Divinely superfluous beauty
Rules the games, presides over destinies, makes trees grow
And hills tower, waves fall.
The incredible beauty of joy.
Stars with fire the joining of lips, O let our loves too
Be joined, there is not a maiden
Burns and thirsts for love
More than my blood for you, by the shore of seals while the wings
Weave like a web in the air
Divinely superfluous beauty.

Robinson Jeffers

ADAM

I take thee now to be no other
than you are. In the raw weather
of Northeast storms, in summer meadows
run with only the seabirds' shadows,

I risk my naked and imperfect praise.
From noon to sunlit moon, the days
make ceremony of my quick desire.
Wave by wave, the gray stone shore

diminishes to sand, the known coast
ebbs: and we stand watching, crest
on blue and whitecap crest, who search
still for a tidal lovers' beach.

Yet never do quivering lovers touch
the secret place they join to reach;
at flood between them, love divides,
as barred islands by spring tides.

So must we, Eve, content ourselves
how close we came. At equinox, our lives
are time enough to love again,
between the loon call and the rain.

And there is world enough. I claim
this coast by giving it a name;
I give you this calm morning
as the first, without storm warning

in the cirrus sky. Fish and seal,
crab and beach pea, breed original
in my mind: heather, starfish forms,
are mine. I love you by the terms

I make to give you. I wake to call
the osprey, tern, the slow-winged gull,
say all the sea's grave names, and build
with words this beach that is the world.

Philip Booth

ANOTHER SONG

And if I say I love you, what of that?
Love is another song that will not sing
Aloud, a beauty made to wonder at
And not to grasp, the breathless fluttering
In the throat. And if I say I love you . . .
Once, in the evening, we played a game—
Do you remember how I ran into
The meadow seeking you, calling your name?
Once when the wind was high and shadows slid
Across the ground, and the white moon was full,
And the hot air was sweet with thyme—I did
Not have to say the night was beautiful.

Oh, if I say I love you, can you know
It better, for my having told you so?

Marion Strobel

A SIMILE FOR HER SMILE

Your smiling, or the hope, the thought of it,
Makes in my mind such pause and abrupt ease
As when the highway bridgegates fall,
Balking the hasty traffic, which must sit
On each side massed and staring, while
Deliberately the drawbridge starts to rise:

Then horns are hushed, the oilsmoke rarefies,
Above the idling motors one can tell
The packet's smooth approach, the slip,
Slip of the silken river past the sides,
The ringing of clear bells, the dip
And slow cascading of the paddle wheel.

Richard Wilbur

SOLITUDES

My heart is a dark forest where no voice is heard,
Nor sound of foot, by day or night—nor echo, borne
Down the long aisles and shadowy arches, of a horn,
Trembling—nor cry of beast, nor call of any bird.

But always through the deep solitudes a grieving wind
Moves, like the voice of a vast prayer: it is your love
Lifting and bending leaf and bough—while, far above,
One thought soars like a hawk, in the heaven of my mind.

John Hall Wheelock

50

REUNION

Night after night I always come to you,
Darkness and distance do not ever divide us;
Nor the rainstorms nor bleak hills nor seas nor lightnings:
We lie together always until dawn,
Cheerfully, joyously, taking love from each other,
Naked as truth are our souls,
Our bodies are naked and pure.

I enter into your house without knocking,
With a smile you always greet me:
I know well you are all the world to me,
You know well I am all the world to you.
We know well we are together,
Love made us one—hate cannot ever change us.

We have not parted and we shall not part.

Night after night I always come to you,
For I have given to you my soul to cherish;
It is lost in you like a ship in the immense ocean.
You are the star to which my course is pointed,
You are the port to which my prow is lifted,
You are the beacon of my nights, the sun of my lone dayspring,
For my soul is safe with you unto eternity,
You will look after it—you will not let it stray aside.

Only to come and take of my soul from your lips,
That is all I need—and I come surely;
I shall be with you night on night for always:
You too will always see your soul in my own eyes.
You will run towards me on glad feet, smiling,
I know you are coming with the lamp, my darling;
Night after night I shall visit you for always:
And in this knowledge I can rest content.

John Gould Fletcher

WHEN IN THE CROWD I SUDDENLY BEHOLD

When in the crowd I suddenly behold
   Your small, proud head, so like a queen for grace,
Bearing its weight of spun and twisted gold
   Like an old crown on an imperial face;
When through the chime of gossip and the cries,
   I meet your glance, amused, serene, and bright
With some small secret, and behold your eyes
   Leap into laughter and immediate light,
Then as a bird might hear repeated over
   (His own song done) the same familiar part
From distant boughs and from the absent lover,
   And with that single beauty fill his heart,
I hear all other sounds, all other words,
Dwindle to silence like the sound of birds.

Robert Nathan

TO A GOLDEN-HAIRED GIRL
IN A LOUISIANA TOWN

You are a sunrise,
If a star should rise instead of the sun.
You are a moonrise,
If a star should come in the place of the moon.
You are the Spring,
If a face should bloom instead of an apple-bough.
You are my love,
If your heart is as kind
As your young eyes now.

Vachel Lindsay

SONNET XXXIII

My only need—you ask me, and I tell you—
Is that henceforth forever you exist.
You are not mine; I may not ever bell you
Like an owned animal for night and mist.
My only need, whatever darkness take me,
Whatever tears close now my separate eyes,
Is that you live, and let the knowledge make me
Immortal as the day that never dies—
That, swift and even, turns into the sun,
As turns the after-shadow down to death.
Let neither then my night, my day be done;
Let them both swing in silence, with no breath
   To call you from the distances you keep.
   Would they were little; would that my love could sleep.

Mark Van Doren

SONNET VI

Chasten your fears, I have not been destroyed,
All that was in me once is living still;
Only I know there was this slender void,
This threading vein through an unconscious hill.
Empty of you, it nourished every part
With nothingness, and I was none the worse.
Filled with you suddenly, it is the start
Of older riches than I can rehearse:
Joy like a hidden river that no stone
Ever is worn away by where it runs;
Peace in the darkest passages of bone,
And buried light as from a hundred suns;
   With tolerance, that sweetens as it flows
   This blood whose red remembers late the rose.

Mark Van Doren

53

THE LAMP

If I can bear your love like a lamp before me,
When I go down the long steep Road of Darkness,
I shall not fear the everlasting shadows,
        Nor cry in terror.

If I can find out God, then I shall find Him,
If none can find Him, then I shall sleep soundly,
Knowing how well on earth your love sufficed me,
        A lamp in darkness.

Sara Teasdale

MIDCENTURY LOVE LETTER

Stay near me. Speak my name. Oh, do not wander
By a thought's span, heart's impulse, from the light
We kindle here. You are my sole defender
(As I am yours) in this precipitous night,
Which over earth, till common landmarks alter,
Is falling, without stars, and bitter cold.
We two have but our burning selves for shelter.
Huddle against me. Give me your hand to hold.

So might two climbers lost in mountain weather
On a high slope and taken by the storm,
Desperate in the darkness, cling together
Under one cloak and breathe each other warm.
Stay near me. Spirit, perishable as bone,
In no such winter can survive alone.

Phyllis McGinley

54

You will come, with your slim, expressive arms,
A poise of the head no sculptor has caught
And nuances spoken with shoulder and neck . . .

DREAM GIRL

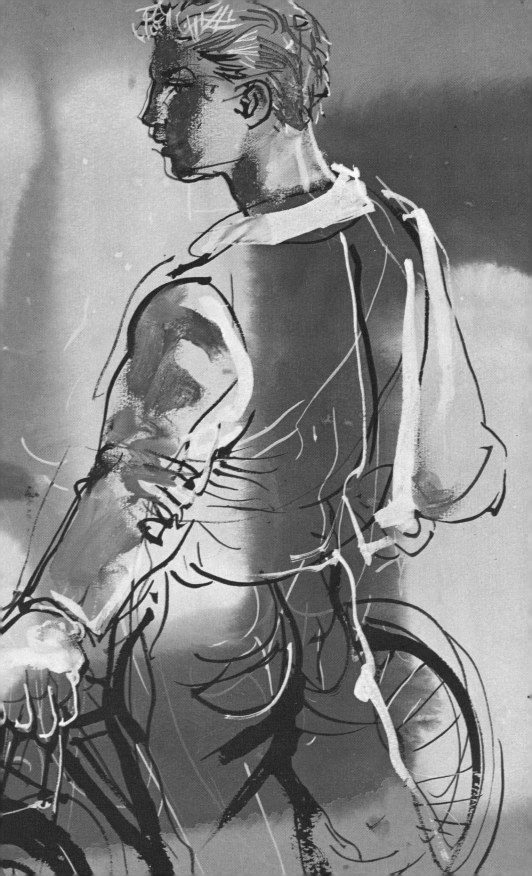

MODERN DECLARATION

I, having loved ever since I was a child a few things, never having
   wavered
In these affections; never through shyness in the houses of the rich
   or in the presence of clergymen having denied these loves;
Never when worked upon by cynics like chiropractors having grunted
   or clicked a vertebra to the discredit of these loves;
Never when anxious to land a job having diminished them by a
   conniving smile; or when befuddled by drink
Jeered at them through heartache or lazily fondled the fingers of
   their alert enemies; declare

That I shall love you always.
No matter what party is in power;
No matter what temporarily expedient combination of allied interests
   wins the war;
Shall love you always.

Edna St. Vincent Millay

COUNTING

Sweet lips, there are songs about kisses now.
Looking backward are kisses of remembrance
Looking ahead are kisses to be wished-for.
So time is counted, so far back, so far ahead, in
   measurements of sweet kisses.

Carl Sandburg

HIPPOCRENE

With you,
    I sup on singing birds
And drink hot sunlight cooled with clouds.

With you,
    I ride the slanting winds,
Toss coloured balls back and forth over the moon,
Swing up through trees,
And slide down swiftly upon beds of irises.

When you are here,
    we stack words at the end of a rainbow
And bowl at them with swans' eggs.

We run races through grass
    to old bronze temples,
And sitting under marble porches,
Count daisy petals
    to the tapping of a bell.

We leap from steeples,
And land in flowered palaces.

In cedar-scented parlours you tell me tales,
Long, slow tales,
    strummed lightly on a lute;
And I lie on blue cushions and watch the sea
    and hear your voice.

With you,
    I do all these things—
How therefore should I care
    to gabble with the donkey-men,
To gossip with the old women
    who sell turkeys,
To watch my next-door neighbour plait her hair
    and lament the untoward price of butter.

Until you come I will sit here
    alone, by a quiet window,
And, with a fine brush,
    trace little pictures
To show when you return.

Amy Lowell

"WHEN I AM NOT WITH YOU"

When I am not with you
I am alone,
For there is no one else
And there is nothing
That comforts me but you.
When you are gone
Suddenly I am sick,
Blackness is round me,
There is nothing left.
I have tried many things,
Music and cities,
Stars in their constellations
And the sea,
But there is nothing
That comforts me but you;
And my poor pride bows down
Like grass in a rain-storm
Drenched with my longing.
The night is unbearable;
Oh let me go to you
For there is no one,
There is nothing
To comfort me but you.

Sara Teasdale

RE-STATEMENT OF ROMANCE

The night knows nothing of the chants of night.
It is what it is as I am what I am:
And in perceiving this I best perceive myself

And you. Only we two may interchange
Each in the other what each has to give.
Only we two are one, not you and night.

Nor night and I, but you and I, alone,
So much alone, so deeply by ourselves,
So far beyond the casual solitudes,

That night is only the background of our selves,
Supremely true each to its separate self,
In the pale light that each upon the other throws.

Wallace Stevens

UNNAMED
from *Paterson*

Better than flowers
is a view of yourself
my darling—

I'm so glad you came
I thought I should never
see you again.

William Carlos Williams

THE GREAT HUNT

I cannot tell you now;
    When the wind's drive and whirl
    Blow me along no longer,
    And the wind's a whisper at last—
Maybe I'll tell you then—
                some other time.

    When the rose's flash to the sunset
    Reels to the rack and the twist,
    And the rose is a red bygone,
    When the face I love is going
    And the gate to the end shall clang,
    And it's no use to beckon or say, "So long"—
Maybe I'll tell you then—
                some other time.

I never knew any more beautiful than you:
    I have hunted you under my thoughts,
    I have broken down under the wind
    And into the roses looking for you.
     I shall never find any
                greater than you.

Carl Sandburg

SONNETS—UNREALITIES
I

it may not always be so; and i say
that if your lips, which i have loved, should touch
another's, and your dear strong fingers clutch
his heart, as mine in time not far away;
if on another's face your sweet hair lay
in such a silence as i know, or such
great writhing words as, uttering overmuch,
stand helplessly before the spirit at bay;

if this should be, i say if this should be—
you of my heart, send me a little word;
that i may go unto him, and take his hands,
saying, Accept all happiness from me.
then shall i turn my face, and hear one bird
sing terribly afar in the lost lands.

e. e. cummings

THE QUARREL

Suddenly, after the quarrel, while we waited,
Disheartened, silent, with downcast looks, nor stirred
Eyelid nor finger, hopeless both, yet hoping
Against all hope to unsay the sundering word:

While all the room's stillness deepened, deepened about us,
And each of us crept his thought's way to discover
How, with as little sound as the fall of a leaf,
The shadow had fallen, and lover quarreled with lover;

And while in the quiet I marveled—alas, alas—
At your deep beauty, your tragic beauty, torn
As the pale flower is torn by the wanton sparrow—
This beauty, pitied and loved, and now forsworn;

It was then, when the instant darkened to it darkest,—
When faith was lost with hope, and the rain conspired
To strike its gray arpeggios against our heartstrings,—
When love no longer dared, and scarcely desired:

It was then that suddenly, in the neighbor's room,
The music started: that brave quartette of strings
Breaking out of the stillness, as out of our stillness,
Like the indomitable heart of life that sings

When all is lost; and startled from our sorrow,
Tranced from our grief by that diviner grief,
We raised remembering eyes, each looked at other,
Blinded with tears of joy; and another leaf

Fell silently as that first; and in the instant
The shadow had gone, our quarrel became absurd;
And we rose, to the angelic voices of the music,
And I touched your hand, and we kissed, without a word.

Conrad Aiken

A LIGHT LEFT ON

In the evening we came back
Into our yellow room,
For a moment taken aback
To find the light left on,
Falling on silent flowers,
Table, book, empty chair
While we had gone elsewhere,
Had been away for hours.

When we came home together
We found the inside weather.
All of our love unended
The quiet light demanded,
And we gave, in a look
At yellow walls and open book.
The deepest world we share
And do not talk about
But have to have, was there,
And by that light found out.

May Sarton

SONG OF THE MIDNIGHT RAIN

There was rain without, and lightning stalked into the room;
But, in our hearts, there was joy that transcended all pain;
The gloom of the midnight grew dense, but through thick
    strands of rain,
We arose as on tense wings of angels over our gloom.

There was song in the night and the thought of you there
    at my side,
Filling my heart with fresh glory, till it forgot every wrong;
The tide of our love rose and fell and its pull was so strong,
That its beauty in us could ever swell and abide.

There was dawn at the last, and the chalice of love drained
    deep,
The clouds through the morning passing, the curtain of close
    night withdrawn.
Outstretched in white beauty you lay at the coming forth
    of the day;
We had wandered all night in the garden, hid behind ram-
    parts of sleep.

John Gould Fletcher

DAYBREAK

At dawn she lay with her profile at that angle
Which, sleeping, seems the stone face of an angel;
Her hair a harp the hand of a breeze follows
To play, against the white cloud of the pillows.
Then in flush of rose she woke, and her eyes were open
Swimming with blue through the rose of dawn.
From her dew of lips, the drop of one word
Fell, from a dawn of fountains, when she murmured
"Darling" upon my heart the song of the first bird.
"My dream glides in my dream," she said, "come true.
I waken from you to my dream of you."
O then my waking dream dared assume
The audacity of her sleep. Our dreams
Flowed into each other's arms, like dreams.

Stephen Spender

THE VOYAGE

The ship of my body has danced in the dance of the storm
And pierced to the center the heavy embrace of the tide;
It has plunged to the bottomless trough with the knife of its form
And leapt with the prow of its motion elate from the bride.

And now in the dawn I am salt with the taste of the wave,
Which lies with itself and suspires, her beauty asleep,
And I peer at the fishes with jaws that devour and rave
And hunt in her dream for the wrack of our hands in the deep.

But the wind is the odor of love that awakes in the sun
The stream of our voyage that lies on the belt of the seas,
And I gather and breathe in the rays of the darkness undone,
And drift in her silence of morning and sail at my ease,

Where the sponges and rubbery seaweeds and flowers of hair
Uprooted abound in the water and choke in the air.

Karl Shapiro

HOLIDAY

Summer was another country, where the birds
Woke us at dawn among the dripping leaves
And lent to all our fêtes their sweet approval.
The touch of air on flesh was lighter, keener,
The senses flourished like a laden tree
Whose every gesture finishes in a flower.
In those unwardened provinces we dined
From wicker baskets by a green canal,
Staining our lips with peach and nectarine,
Slapping at golden wasps. And when we kissed,
Tasting that sunlit juice, the landscape folded
Into our clasp, and not a breath recalled
The long walk back to winter, leagues away.

Adrienne Cecile Rich

OUT OF THE SEA

With your sun-white hair and your smile
And your body as white as a white sea-bird,
I took you and held you and watched you awhile
    And never a word.

Nothing to say, to explain
Or to answer, nothing to hear or be heard,
Only to kiss you again and again
    With never a word.

Even lately I cannot be sure.
It seems in my sleep that we neither have stirred,
So silent you vanished, so sweet you endure,
    And never a word.

Witter Bynner

THE HILL

Breathless, we flung us on the windy hill,
    Laughed in the sun, and kissed the lovely grass.
    You said, "Through glory and ecstasy we pass;
Wind, sun, and earth remain, the birds sing still,
When we are old, are old. . . ." "And when we die
    All's over that is ours: and life burns on
Through other lovers, other lips," said I,
—"Heart of my heart, our heaven is now, is won!"

"We are Earth's best, that learnt her lesson here.
Life is our cry. We have kept the faith!" we said;
    "We shall go down with unreluctant tread
Rose-crowned into the darkness!" . . . Proud we were,
And laughed, that had such brave true things to say.
—And then you suddenly cried, and turned away.

Rupert Brooke

YOUR BODY IS STARS

Your body is stars whose million glitter here:
I am lost among the branches of this sky
Here near my breast, here in my nostrils, here
Where our vast arms like streams of fire lie.

How can this end? My healing fills the night
And hangs its flags in worlds I cannot near.
Our movements range through miles, and when we kiss
The moment widens to enclose the years.

. . .

Beholders of the promised dawn of truth,
The explorers of immense and simple lines,
Here is our goal, men cried, but it was lost
Amongst the mountain mists and mountain pines.

So with this face of love, whose breathings are
A mystery shadowed on the desert floor:
The promise hangs, this swarm of stars and flowers,
And then there comes the shutting of a door.

Stephen Spender

SECOND NIGHT, OR WHAT YOU WILL

Say, "You are lovely!", say
"Your body's beautiful!"
And nothing left to say
Nor any more to do
But tremble in the dark
Between the flesh and wall.

Lights out, and only light
From the street corner thrown
Across the naked breast;
Hair dark, and lip at rest
Parted from that delight:
The body tried and taken,
The still unproven mind,
O incompletely known!

Who but ourselves will ever
To or from this deliver
Wholly the flesh and mind
To break or stay in season?
Time will not shift in favor,
Nor circumstance be kind.

Rolfe Humphries

DEFINITION

This fullness that is emptiness,
This hunger that is food;
This union, solitariness,
This wild air, this warm blood;
This poverty, and rich sensation,
This haste, this slow growing,
True marriage, separation,
All-knowing that is not-knowing;
Late fulfillment, early death,
This huge passion, this small breath.

May Sarton

LOVE

Love is a breach in the walls, a broken gate,
    Where that comes in that shall not go again;
Love sells the proud heart's citadel to Fate.
    They have known shame, who love unloved. Even then,
When two mouths, thirsty each for each, find slaking,
    And agony's forgot, and hushed the crying
Of credulous hearts, in heaven—such are but taking
    Their own poor dreams within their arms, and lying
Each in his lonely night, each with a ghost
    Some share that night. But they know love grows colder,
Grows false and dull, that was sweet lies at most.
    Astonishment is no more in hand or shoulder,
But darkens, and dies out from kiss to kiss.
All this is love; and all love is but this.

Rupert Brooke

PSYCHE WITH THE CANDLE

Love which is the most difficult mystery
Asking from every young one answers
And most from those most eager and most beautiful—
Love is a bird in a fist:
To hold it hides it, to look at it lets it go.
It will twist loose if you lift so much as a finger.
It will stay if you cover it—stay but unknown and invisible.
Either you keep it forever with fist closed
Or let it fling
Singing in fervor of sun and in song vanish.
There is no answer other to this mystery.

Archibald MacLeish

DOGMA

Love is not true: mathematicians know
Truth, that's alive in heaven, and in the mind—
Out of our bodies; you will never find
Love strict as number, and enduring so.
It is not free: alone the grave's narrower
Than the little space in which this passion moves,
With a door that opens inward: he who loves
Measures his paces like a prisoner.

They who give it large names are liars, or
They are fools. More softly, you and I,
Slow to assert what we can never prove,
Wonder what algebraist, what dictator
Can teach us much of truth or tyranny.
Look at me. Do not speak. But this is love.

Babette Deutsch

HANDS

Strange, how this smooth and supple joint can be
    Put to so many purposes. It checks
And rears the monsters of machinery
    And shapes the idle gallantries of sex.

Those hands that light the fuse and dig the trap,
    Fingers that spin the earth or plunge through shame—
And yours, that lie so lightly in your lap,
    And only blood and dust—all are the same.

What mastery directs them through the world
    And gives these delicate bones so great a power? . . .
You drop your head. You sleep. Your hands are curled
    Loosely, like some half-opened, perfumed flower.

An hour ago they burned in mine and sent
    Armies with banners charging through my veins.
Now they are cool and white; they rest content,
    Curved in a smile. The mystery remains.

                    Louis Untermeyer

UNNAMED
from *Paterson*

    Your lovely hands
    Your lovely tender hands!
    Reflections of what grace
    what heavenly joy

    predicted for the world
    in knowing you—
    blest, as am I, and humbled
    by such ecstasy.

            William Carlos Williams

LOVE FOR A HAND

Two hands lie still, the hairy and the white,
And soon down ladders of reflected light
The sleepers climb in silence. Gradually
They separate on paths of long ago,
Each winding on his arm the unpleasant clew
That leads, live as a nerve, to memory.

But often when too steep her dream descends,
Perhaps to the grotto where her father bends
To pick her up, the husband wakes as though
He had forgotten something in the house.
Motionless he eyes the room that glows
With the little animals of light that prowl

This way and that. Soft are the beasts of light
But softer still her hand that drifts so white
Upon the whiteness. How like a water-plant
It floats upon the black canal of sleep,
Suspended upward from the distant deep
In pure achievement of its lovely want!

Quietly then he plucks it and it folds
And is again a hand, small as a child's.
He would revive it but it barely stirs
And so he carries it off a little way
And breaks it open gently. Now he can see
The sweetness of the fruit, his hand eats hers.

Karl Shapiro

BY MOONLIGHT

We are true lovers without hope
Whose hearts are locked to time,
So lie with me on the grassy sward
On the cool black-shadowed slope,
For we'll not sleep in a close warm room:
Whatever we are moving toward
An ample bed's not our reward
Who are mad with the moon.

Wherever passionate love is leading
We'll be discovering alone,
So little hope it can endure,
So wild, so deep, so dark the needing
That even fastened bone to bone,
We'll not have lasting peace, that's sure,
Nor any haven from despair
Who love by light of moon.

So come, though we shall never rest
In any house to call our own,
By any hearth we light and tend,
Lie here upon the cold earth's breast
And lean your length hard on the stone:
Hearts break and they may also mend
But here until the certain end,
Wed me by light of moon.

Now the great open sky is ours
And the long light across the loam,
And we, gigantic hearts of dust,
Lie open like night-blooming flowers.
The homeless moon is our bright home,
And we shine too because we must,
Oh magic that we cannot trust,
The lovely changing moon!

May Sarton

78

THE WALK ON THE BEACH

The evening, blue, voluptuous, of June
Settled slowly on the beach with pulsating wings,
Like a sea-gull come to rest: far, far off twinkled
Gold lights from the towers of a city and a passing ship.
The dark sea rolled its body at the end of the beach,
The warm soft beach which it was too tired to climb,
And we two walked together there
Arm in arm, having nothing in our souls but love.

Your face shaded by the hat looked up at me;
Your pale face framed in the dark gold of your hair,
Your face with its dumb unforgettable look in the eyes,
A look I have only once seen, that I shall see never again.
Our steps were lost on the long vast carpet of sand,
Our souls were lost in the sky where the stars came out;
Our bodies clung together: time was not.
Love came and passed: our lives were cleaned and changed.

The winter will spill upon us soon its dark cruse laden with rain,
Time has broken our moorings; we have drifted apart; love is done.
I can only dream in the long still nights that we rest heart to heart,
I can only wake to the knowledge that my love is lost and won.
We were as two weak swallows, together to southward set,
Blown apart, vainly crying to each other while at strife with the seas.
We go out in the darkness; we speak but in memories;
But I have never forgotten and I shall never forget.

John Gould Fletcher

FROM THE SEA

All beauty calls you to me, and you seem,
Past twice a thousand miles of shifting sea,
To reach me. You are as the wind I breathe
Here on the ship's sun-smitten topmost deck,
With only light between the heavens and me.
I feel your spirit and I close my eyes,
Knowing the bright hair blowing in the sun,
The eager whisper and the searching eyes.

   * * * * * *

Listen, I love you. Do not turn your face
Nor touch me. Only stand and watch awhile
The blue unbroken circle of the sea.
Look far away and let me ease my heart
Of words that beat in it with broken wing.
Look far away, and if I say too much,
Forget that I am speaking. Only watch,
How like a gull that sparkling sinks to rest,
The foam-crest drifts along a happy wave
Toward the bright verge, the boundary of the world.

   * * * * * *

I am so weak a thing, praise me for this,
That in some strange way I was strong enough
To keep my love unuttered and to stand
Altho' I longed to kneel to you that night
You looked at me with ever-calling eyes.
Was I not calm? And if you guessed my love
You thought it something delicate and free,
Soft as the sound of fir-trees in the wind,
Fleeting as phosphorescent stars in foam.
Yet in my heart there was a beating storm
Bending my thoughts before it, and I strove
To say too little lest I say too much,
And from my eyes to drive love's happy shame.
Yet when I heard your name the first far time
It seemed like other names to me, and I

Was all unconscious, as a dreaming river
That nears at last its long predestined sea;
And when you spoke to me, I did not know
That to my life's high altar came its priest.
But now I know between my God and me
You stand forever, nearer God than I,
And in your hands with faith and utter joy
I would that I could lay my woman's soul.

      *   *   *   *   *   *

Oh, my love
To whom I cannot come with any gift
Of body or of soul, I pass and go.
But sometimes when you hear blown back to you
My wistful, far-off singing touched with tears,
Know that I sang for you alone to hear,
And that I wondered if the wind would bring
To him who tuned my heart its distant song.
So might a woman who in loneliness
Had borne a child, dreaming of days to come,
Wonder if it would please its father's eyes.
But long before I ever heard your name,
Always the undertone's unchanging note
In all my singing had prefigured you,
Foretold you as a spark foretells a flame.
Yet I was free as an untethered cloud
In the great space between the sky and sea,
And might have blown before the wind of joy
Like a bright banner woven by the sun.
I did not know the longing in the night—
You who have waked me cannot give me sleep.
All things in all the world can rest, but I,
Even the smooth brief respite of a wave
When it gives up its broken crown of foam,
Even that little rest I may not have.
And yet all quiet loves of friends, all joy
In all the piercing beauty of the world
I would give up—go blind forevermore,
Rather than have God blot from out my soul
Remembrance of your voice that said my name.

For us no starlight stilled the April fields,
No birds awoke in darkling trees for us,
Yet where we walked the city's street that night
Felt in our feet the singing fire of spring,
And in our path we left a trail of light
Soft as the phosphorescence of the sea
When night submerges in the vessel's wake
A heaven of unborn evanescent stars.

Sara Teasdale

SONNET XIV

I was confused; I cannot promise more
This morning than to keep these miles between us.
I can do that, although the heart grow sore
And the night weep for ever having seen us.
I can do that; but I will not engage
To come and slay this love before your eyes.
Let it die here, without the extra wage
Of torture that would shame us everywise.
Let me come afterward, however long,
And say to you I love you none the less.
Nor will I speak of any righted wrong.
Let it be dead, and let us both confess
      With laughter how we fasted forty days
      In the kind wilderness of time's delays.

Mark Van Doren

How strange it is that only such gentleness
Begets the fury of joy and all its tenderness . . .

HOW STRANGE LOVE IS, IN EVERY STATE OF CONSCIOUSNESS

THE DARK CHAMBER

The brain forgets, but the blood will remember.
    There, when the play of sense is over,
The last, low spark in the darkest chamber
    Will hold all there is of love and lover.

The war of words, the life-long quarrel
    Of self against self will resolve into nothing;
Less than the chain of berry-red coral
    Crying against the dead black of her clothing.

What has the brain that it hopes to last longer?
    The blood will take from forgotten violence,
The groping, the break of her voice in anger.
    There will be left only color and silence.

These will remain, these will go searching
    Your veins for life when the flame of life smoulders:
The night that you two saw the mountains marching
    Up against dawn with the stars on their shoulders—

The jetting poplars' arrested fountains
    As you drew her under them, easing her pain—
The notes, not the words, of a half-finished sentence—
    The music, the silence . . . these will remain.

Louis Untermeyer

SPOILS

When all is over and you march for home,
The spoils of war are easily disposed of:
Standards, weapons of combat, helmets, drums
May decorate a staircase or a study,
While lesser gleanings of the battlefield—
Coins, watches, wedding-rings, gold teeth and such—
Are sold anonymously for solid cash.

The spoils of love present a different case,
When all is over and you march for home:
That lock of hair, those letters and the portrait
May not be publicly displayed; nor sold;
Nor burned; nor returned (the heart being obstinate)—
Yet never dare entrust them to a safe
For fear they burn a hole through two-foot steel.

Robert Graves

I. THIS LITTLE VIGIL

Between the first pangs and the last of love
There is no difference, but that the first
Are bitter-sweet, the last are merely bitter.

Here in the waste of fore and after desert
The brief oasis of a trysting passage
Lures to the longed-for and regretted joys.

Charles G. Bell

FORE THOUGHT

What is left at the end?
Shape of a mouth or a hand,
Something not understood
That they must understand?
Nothing left at the end,
Not a breath or a touch:
These lovers loved so much
All was consumed. Desire
Burned itself in the fire.
When they arise estranged,
When nothing's left to burn,
And coldness at the bone,
No, they will not return.
They will stand up full-grown,
And love itself be changed
To walk the earth alone.

May Sarton

CARREFOUR

O you,
Who came upon me once
Stretched under apple-trees just after bathing,
Why did you not strangle me before speaking
Rather than fill me with the wild white honey of your words
And then leave me to the mercy
Of the forest bees.

Amy Lowell

A SEPARATION

Yes. The will decided. But how can the heart decide,
Lying deep under the surface
Of the level reasons the eye sees—
How can the heart decide
To banish this loved face for ever?

The starry eyes reeded with darkness
To forgo? The light within the body's blindness?
To prove that these were lost in any case
And accept the stumbling stumps of consolation?

Under sleep, under day,
Under the earth, in the tunnel of the marrow,
Unchanging love swears all's unchanged, and knows
That what it has not, still stays all it has.

Stephen Spender

CHAMBER MUSIC XXVIII

Gentle lady, do not sing
    Sad songs about the end of love;
Lay aside sadness and sing
    How love that passes is enough.

Sing about the long deep sleep
    Of lovers that are dead, and how
In the grave all love shall sleep:
    Love is aweary now.

James Joyce

NEVER GIVE ALL THE HEART

Never give all the heart, for love
Will hardly seem worth thinking of
To passionate women if it seem
Certain, and they never dream
That it fades out from kiss to kiss;
For everything that's lovely is
But a brief, dreamy, kind delight.
O never give the heart outright,
For they, for all smooth lips can say,
Have given their hearts up to the play.
And who could play it well enough
If deaf and dumb and blind with love?
He that made this knows all the cost,
For he gave all his heart and lost.

William Butler Yeats

WHEN YOU ARE OLD

When you are old and grey and full of sleep,
And nodding by the fire, take down this book,
And slowly read, and dream of the soft look
Your eyes had once, and of their shadows deep;

How many loved your moments of glad grace,
And loved your beauty with love false or true,
But one man loved the pilgrim soul in you,
And loved the sorrows of your changing face;

And bending down beside the glowing bars,
Murmur, a little sadly, how Love fled
And paced upon the mountains overhead
And hid his face amid a crowd of stars.

William Butler Yeats

THE NEW RING

The new ring oppresses the finger, embarrasses the hand, encumbers the whole arm. The free hand moves to cover the new ring, except late-at-night when the mouth reaches to kiss the soft silver, a sudden thought.

In the lodge of marriage, the secret society of love, the perfect circle binds and separates, moves and is stationary.

Till the ring becomes the flesh, leaving a white trench, and the finger is immune. For the brand is assumed. Till the flesh of the encumbered hand grows over the ring, as living wood over and around the iron spike. Till the value of the reason of the gift is coin-worn, and the wound heals.

And until the wound heals, the new ring is a new nail driven through the hand upon the living wood, and the body hangs from the nail, and the nail holds.

Karl Shapiro

MARRIAGE

No wandering any more where the feet stumble
Upon a sudden rise, or sink in damp
Marsh grasses. No uncertain following on
With nothing there to follow: a sure bird,
A fence, a farmhouse. No adventuring now
Where motion that is yet not motion dies.
Circles have lost their magic, and the voice
Comes back upon itself. The road is firm.
It runs, and the dust is not too deep, and the end
Never can heave in sight, though one is there.
It runs in a straight silence, till a word
Turns it; then a sentence, and evening falls
At an expected inn, whose barest room
Cannot be lonely with the walls forgotten.
Laughter is morning, and the road resumes;
Adventurous, it never will return.

Mark Van Doren

TO JUDITH ASLEEP

My dear, darkened in sleep, turned from the moon
that riots on curtain-stir with every breeze,
leaping in moths of light across your back . . .
far off, then soft and sudden as petals shower
down from wired roses—silently, all at once—
you turn, abandoned and naked, all let down
in ferny streams of sleep and petaled thighs
rippling into my flesh's buzzing garden.

Far and familiar your body's myth-map lights,
traveled by moon and dapple. Sagas were curved
like scimitars to your hips. The raiders' ships
all sailed to your one port. And watchfires burned
your image on the hills. Sweetly you drown
male centuries in your chiaroscuro tide
of breast and breath. And all my memory's shores
you frighten perfectly, washed familiar and far.

Ritual wars have climbed your shadowed flank
where bravos dreaming of fair women tore
rock out of rock to have your cities down
in loot of hearths and trophies of desire.
And desert monks have fought your image back
in a hysteria of mad skeletons.
Bravo and monk (the heads and tails of love)
I stand, a spinning coin of wish and dread,

Counting our life, our chairs, our books and walls,
our clock whose radium eye and insect voice
owns all our light and shade, and your white shell
spiraled in moonlight on the bed's white beach;
thinking, I might press you to my ear
And all your coils fall out in sounds of surf
washing a mystery sudden as you are
a light on light in light beyond the light.

Child, child, and making legend of my wish
fastened alive into your naked sprawl—
stir once to stop my fear and miser's panic
that time shall have you last and legendry
undress to old bones from its moon brocade.
Yet sleep and keep our prime of time alive
before that death of legend. My dear of all

saga and century, sleep in familiar-far.
Time still must tick *this is, I am, we are.*

John Ciardi

V-LETTER

I love you first because your face is fair,
    Because your eyes Jewish and blue,
Set sweetly with the touch of foreignness
Above the cheekbones, stare rather than dream.
Often your countenance recalls a boy
    Blue-eyed and small, whose silent mischief
Tortured his parents and compelled my hate
    To wish his ugly death.
Because of this reminder, my soul's trouble,
And for your face, so often beautiful,
    I love you, wish you life.

I love you first because you wait, because
    For your own sake, I cannot write
Beyond these words. I love you for these words
That sting and creep like insects and leave filth.
I love you for the poverty you cry
    And I bend down with tears of steel
That melt your hand like wax, not for this war
    The droplets shattering
Those candle-glowing fingers of my joy,
But for your name of agony, my love,
    That cakes my mouth with salt.

And all your imperfections and perfections
    And all your magnitude of grace
And all this love explained and unexplained
Is just a breath. I see you woman-size
And this looms larger and more goddess-like
    Than silver goddesses on screens.
I see you in the ugliness of light,
    Yet you are beautiful,
And in the dark of absence your full length
Is such as meets my body to the full
    Though I am starved and huge.

You turn me from these days as from a scene
    Out of an open window far
Where lies the foreign city and the war.
You are my home and in your spacious love
I dream to march as under flaring flags
    Until the door is gently shut.
Give me the tearless lesson of your pride,
        Teach me to live and die
As one deserving anonymity,
The mere devotion of a house to keep
        A woman and a man.

Give me the free and poor inheritance
    Of our own kind, not furniture
Of education, nor the prophet's pose,
The general cause of words, the hero's stance,
The ambitions incommensurable with flesh,
    But the drab makings of a room
Where sometimes in the afternoon of thought
        The brief and blinding flash
May light the enormous chambers of your will
And show the gracious Parthenon that time
        Is ever measured by.

As groceries in a pantry gleam and smile
    Because they are important weights
Bought with the metal minutes of your pay,
So do these hours stand in solid rows,
The dowry for a use in common life.
    I love you first because your years
Lead to my matter-of-fact and simple death
        Or to our open marriage,
And I pray nothing for my saftey back,
Not even luck, because our love is whole
        Whether I live or fail.

                                    Karl Shapiro

MEN MARRY WHAT THEY NEED. I MARRY YOU

Men marry what they need. I marry you,
morning by morning, day by day, night by night,
and every marriage makes this marriage new.

In the broken name of heaven, in the light
that shatters granite, by the spitting shore,
in air that leaps and wobbles like a kite,

I marry you from time and a great door
is shut and stays shut against wind, sea, stone,
sunburst, and heavenfall. And home once more

inside our walls of skin and struts of bone,
man-woman, woman-man, and each the other,
I marry you by all dark and all dawn

and learn to let time spend. Why should I bother
the flies about me? Let them buzz and do.
Men marry their queen, their daughter, or their mother

by names they prove, but that thin buzz whines through:
when reason falls to reasons, cause is true.
Men marry what they need. I marry you.

John Ciardi

MOST LIKE AN ARCH THIS MARRIAGE

Most like an arch—an entrance which upholds
and shores the stone-crush up the air like lace.
Mass made idea, and idea held in place.
A lock in time. Inside half-heaven unfolds.

Most like an arch—two weaknesses that lean
into a strength. Two fallings become firm.
Two joined abeyances become a term
naming the fact that teaches fact to mean.

Not quite that? Not much less. World as it is,
what's strong and separate falters. All I do
at piling stone on stone apart from you
is roofless around nothing. Till we kiss

I am no more than upright and unset.
It is by falling in and in we make
the all-bearing point, for one another's sake,
in faultless failing, raised by our own weight.

John Ciardi

MARRIAGE: TO K.

When in the bedded dark of night
I touch your body huddled tight,

Though each is singular and free
In numerous humanity,

I have some special knowledge then
That crosses and will cross again.

Donald Hall

POEM IN PROSE

This poem if for my wife.
I have made it plainly and honestly:
The mark is on it
Like the burl on the knife.

I have not made it for praise.
She has no more need for praise
Than summer has
Or the bright days.

In all that becomes a woman
Her words and her ways are beautiful:
Love's lovely duty,
The well-swept room.

Wherever she is there is sun
And time and a sweet air:
Peace is there,
Work done.

There are always curtains and flowers
And candles and baked bread
And a cloth spread
And a clean house.

Her voice when she sings is a voice
At dawn by a freshening sea
Where the wave leaps in the
Wind and rejoices.

Wherever she is it is now.
It is here where the apples are:
Here in the stars,
In the quick hour.

The greatest and richest good,
My own life to live in,
This she has given me—

If giver could.

Archibald MacLeish

THE THINKER

My wife's new pink slippers
have gay pom-poms.
There is not a spot or a stain
on their satin toes or their sides.
All night they lie together
under her bed's edge.
Shivering I catch sight of them
and smile, in the morning.
Later I watch them
descending the stair,
hurrying through the doors
and round the table,
moving stiffly
with a shake of their gay pom-poms!
And I talk to them
in my secret mind
out of pure happiness.

William Carlos Williams

PART OF PLENTY

When she carries food to the table and stoops down
—Doing this out of love—and lays soup with its good
Tickling smell, or fry winking from the fire
And I look up, perhaps from a book I am reading
Or other work: there is an importance of beauty
Which can't be accounted for by there and then,
And attacks me, but not separately from the welcome
Of the food, or the grace of her arms.

When she puts a sheaf of tulips in a jug
And pours in water and presses to one side
The upright stems and leaves that you hear creak,
Or loosens them, or holds them up to show me,
So that I see the tangle of their necks and cups
With the curls of her hair, and the body they are held
Against, and the stalk of the small waist rising
And flowering in the shape of breasts;

Whether in the bringing of the flowers or the food
She offers plenty, and is part of plenty,
And whether I see her stooping, or leaning with the flowers,
What she does is ages old, and she is not simply,
No, but lovely in that way.

Bernard Spencer

OF THE UNSCATHING FIRE

Sitting in our garden you cannot escape symbols,
      Take them how you will.
    Here on the lawn like an island where the wind is still,
      Circled by tides in the field and swirling trees
      It is of love I muse:
This designs the coloured fronds and heavy umbels,
        Second-hand marriage, not for passion but business,
      Brought on by the obliging bees.

This hedge is a cool perch for the brown turtle-dove
        His phoenix unseen:
    Such was their love that they had grown into one;
      At first the mystical making one in marriage
      Had all my heart and my homage:
A fire and a fusion were what I wanted of love,
        But bodies are separate, and her fanatic bliss
      Left the phoenix bodiless.

Frosty burning cloud, delectable gate
      Of heaven hopelessly far,
   Though tilting almost to touch, whose holy fire
      Has no corrosive property unless
      Despair of it destroys us;
When we love, towards you our faces are set.
        Once I would win by the pain of passion alone,
      Aim at you still, that method outgrown.

If daily love now takes from these earlier ones
      The sweetness without the pain,
    The burning nights, the breathless fears gone,
      Peace in their place I never hoped to be given
      Unless at last in Heaven;
It is your doing, my darling, who have at once
        The unscathing fire and the ease of peace,
      All that I praise and bless.

Anne Ridler

LONELY LOVER

Maybe the men on little northern farms
Are tenderer with new-born calves they hold
Because new calves are few and far between,
Because the nights around them are so cold;
The starry-eyed newcomer faces stars
Cold and aloof beyond the frosty bars,
And it takes love to make him brave and bold.

Yet there might be a deeper reason still
Why northern farmers make so much of their stock
And linger on so long after they milk,
Stroking the cow and making soothing talk,
Caressing the ears on the little heifer calf,
Rousing her up to have the chance to laugh
At her coquettish but uncertain walk.

Maybe the man under cold northern skies
Finds in his barn a warmth not in his house;
Things may be too sensibly managed there,
And so he looks for solace out with his cows;
Here he finds a place for his caresses,
Here he lets out pent-up tendernesses
And plays the lonely lover under his mows.

Robert P. Tristram Coffin

THE WIDOW'S LAMENT IN SPRINGTIME

Sorrow is my own yard
where the new grass
flames as it has flamed
often before but not
with the cold fire
that closes round me this year.
Thirtyfive years
I lived with my husband.
The plumtree is white today
with masses of flowers.
Masses of flowers
load the cherry branches
and color some bushes
yellow and some red
but the grief in my heart
is stronger than they
for though they were my joy
formerly, today I notice them
and turned away forgetting.
Today my son told me
that in the meadows,
at the edge of the heavy woods
in the distance, he saw
trees of white flowers.
I feel that I would like
to go there
and fall into those flowers
and sink into the marsh near them.

William Carlos Williams

OLD FARMER ALONE

His hearing left him twenty years ago,
Before his wife went out below the snow
And left him all her quilts and comforters.
He has inherited that room of hers,
The kitchen, where she lived and cooked her way
Into the thoughts he had by night and day.
His being deaf had made him miss her less
When she went, he changed one loneliness
For another, old silence for a new,
He took over things she tended to
In her kitchen with her pots and pans.
His cooking is the kind that is a man's,
And he eats off the stove what he has cooked.

Some nights his first year all alone he looked
Up from eating just as though she might
Be coming home from somewhere in the night,
And he would be ashamed of his not waiting.
The room seemed very large to him, the grating
Let the firelight out upon the wall,
He missed her shadow there the most of all.

But now he never looks up at the place,
He sits and eats and never turns his face
Any night towards the outside door;
And yet, somehow, he misses her the more.
His mind confuses things, and he will sit
Quiet, and be very sure of it,
Sure that when he goes his way to bed,
Shielding the lamp-globe level with his head,
And turns the quilts back, he will find her keeping
A warm place there for him and love and sleeping.

Robert P. Tristram Coffin

106

INDEX OF TITLES

INDEX OF AUTHORS

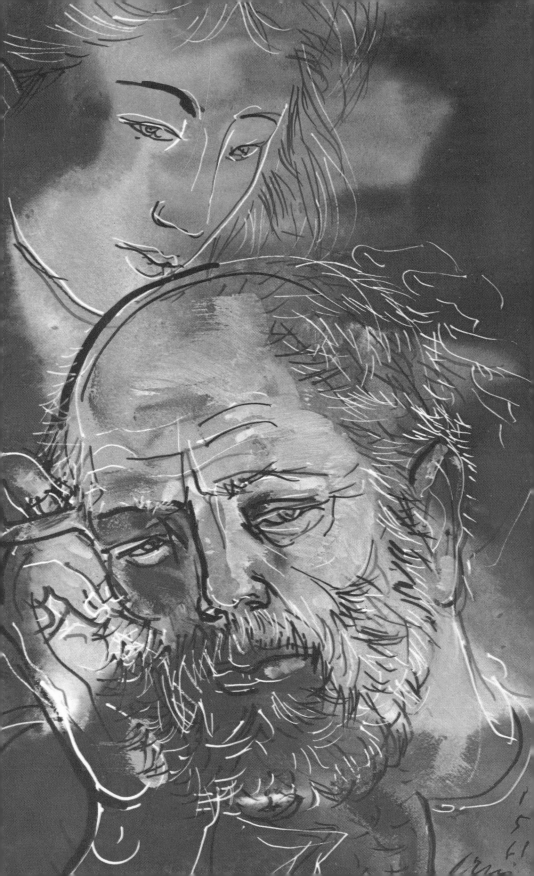

His hearing left him twenty years ago,
Before his wife went out below the snow
And left him all her quilts and comforters.

OLD FARMER ALONE